|| Dedicate to All Plant Lovers Around the World ||

AYURVEDIC REMEDIES FROM THE GARDEN

A GUIDE TO 108 MEDICINAL PLANTS

DR. JAGADEESH PILLAI

Contents

Contents

Contents

Contents

Contents

Contents

Prayer

ōṃ namō bhagavatē vāsudēvāya

dhanvantarayē amṛtakalaśahastāya

[vajrajalaukahastāya]
sarvāmayavināśanāya

trailōkyanāthāya śrīmahāviṣṇavē svāhā ।

☙☙☙

About The Author

Dr. Jagadeesh Pillai is a renowned Guinness World Record holder, writer, and researcher hailing from Varanasi, also known as the abode of Lord Shiva. With a Ph.D. in Vedic Science and a range of creative ideas and achievements, he is a true polymath. Although his roots can be traced back to Kerala, the people of Varanasi hold him in high regard and affectionately consider him one of their own.

Dr. Pillai has achieved four Guinness World Records in the following subjects:

1. "Script to Screen" - In this record, Dr. Pillai produced and directed an animation film within the shortest time possible, breaking the previous record set by Canadians. He has also received numerous national and international awards and recognitions for this achievement.
2. Longest Line of Postcards - For this record, Dr. Pillai created a line of 16,300 postcards on the occasion of the 163rd anniversary of Indian Postal Day. The event also included a questionnaire about the Indian flag.
3. Largest Poster Awareness Campaign - Dr. Pillai designed an awareness campaign on the subject of "Beti Bachao - Beti Padhao" (Save the Girl Child - Educate the Girl Child) to achieve this record.
4. Largest Envelope - In tribute to the Indian Prime Minister's "Make in India" initiative, Dr. Pillai created a 4000 square meter envelope using waste paper to achieve this record.
5. Attempted - 70000 Candles on a 210 kg Cake - To

celebrate the 70th Indian Independence Day, Dr. Pillai attempted to light 70,000 candles on a 210 kg cake, which was recorded in World Records India.

6. Attempted - Documentary on Dhamek Stupa of Sarnath in 17 Languages - Dr. Pillai attempted to create a documentary on the Dhamek Stupa of Sarnath, dubbing it in 17 different languages. The result of this attempt is currently awaiting confirmation from the Guinness World Records.

He is versatile in Gita teaching. The young generation is fond of his Gita teaching and he has changed the life of many young through his continued motivational boost up and teachings.

He has composed and sung Gayatri Mantra in 1008 different tunes.

He has composed and sung Hanuman Chalisa in 108 different tunes.

He has composed and sung hundreds of Sanskrit Bhajans, Patriotic songs, etc.

He has written and directed so many short films and documentaries for awareness campaigns.

He has done voluntary services to UP Police and Kerala Police to spread awareness campaigns on the various issue through videos and photography.

He is on the path of authoring thousands of books on

Indian culture, Indian Temples, and the life of extraordinary people.

It is hard to believe that he has produced and directed more than 100 Documentaries on a particular city (Varanasi) which is done by a single person.

He has helped and guided more than 25 boys and girls to achieve world records through various creative and innovative methods.

A multifaceted person who can apply the best of his intellect using the God-given blessings which have been showered upon every human being granting them an immense capacity to learn, experience, and experiment with many things and do wonders in this world of discrimination and disparities.

He is a teacher and a student at the same time who always learns every day and teaches every day. As a master, his weakness was that he never sticks to a particular subject. Perhaps this weakness gives him the strength to master any area which he came across.

Each of his days dawned with learning a new topic and he spend most of his time experimenting and researching it.

He is also a selfless social activist and a motivational speaker.

His life was full of struggle, ups and downs, and failures. But he never gave up and faced all his trials and tribulations full of confidence. Today he is a successful young man with a lot of enthusiasm and rich life experience.

He is an efficient Tarot Card Reader, Astro-Vastu Consultant and an excellent singer and composer.

He has sung full Ram Charita Manas 138 hours audio by his own composition. He has also sung the whole Bhagavad-Gita in his own composition with a rhythmic background.

He has also sung "Lokah Samastha Sukhino Bhavantu" in 50 different languages.

Currently working on a detailed and scientific study on Veda, Upanishad, Puranas, Bhagavad Gita, etc.

He has composed and sung Hanuman Chalisa in 108 different compositions and Gayatri Mantra in 1008 different compositions.

Awards

Four Times Guinness World Records, Winner of Mahatma Gandhi Vishwa Shanti Puraskar , Mahatma Gandhi Global Peace Ambassador, Kashi Ratna Award, Dr. APJ Abdul Kalam Motivational Person of the Year 2017, Mother Teresa Award, Indira Gandhi Priyadarshini Award, Bharat Vikas Ratna Award, Udyog Ratna Award, Vigyan Prasar Award, Poorvanchal Ratn Samman.

❧❧❧

Preface

The ancient Indian medical system of Ayurveda has been practiced for over 5,000 years and is founded on the belief that health and wellness depend on a delicate balance between the mind, body, and spirit. At the heart of Ayurveda is the use of natural remedies, including herbal medicine.

This book is a guide to 108 of the most commonly used Ayurvedic medicinal plants. Each plant is described in detail, with information on its traditional uses, medicinal properties. In addition to being a valuable resource for those interested in natural remedies and holistic healing, this book is also a testament to the rich and diverse herbal tradition of Ayurveda.

The plants included in this book have been carefully selected based on their long history of use in Ayurvedic medicine and their demonstrated effectiveness in supporting health and well-being. From the humble neem tree, known for its medicinal properties and used to treat a wide range of ailments, to the revered tulsi, or holy basil, revered for its spiritual and physical benefits, these 108 plants represent the breadth and depth of Ayurvedic herbal medicine.

Learn about 108 plus more Ayurvedic medicinal plants in this comprehensive guide. With traditional uses and medicinal properties, this book is a valuable resource for quick reference. Discover the names and origins of these plants, as well as brief information for easy reference. This book is also perfect for those interested in creating a medicinal plant garden.

❦❦❦

Disclaimer

"The purpose of this book is to provide a list of ayurvedic medicinal plants and their origins. The information on the medicinal uses and other properties of these plants has been compiled from various sources, including books and the internet, written by various ayurvedic professionals. It is important to note that this book is intended for informational purposes only and is not a substitute for professional medical advice. We recommend consulting with a qualified healthcare professional before using any of the medicinal plants listed in this book for the treatment of any disease or condition. The intention of creating this book and presenting information on ayurvedic medicinal plants is to fulfill the requests of individuals who wish to create a medicinal garden with these plants. We hope that this information will be useful in guiding your plant selection and usage."

ONE

ARJUNA

Arjuna (अर्जुन) - Terminalia arjuna

Arjuna is a tree native to India, and its bark has been used in Ayurveda for centuries as a natural treatment for a variety of ailments, including heart conditions and poor circulation. It is believed to have antioxidant and anti-inflammatory properties, and it is commonly used to support healthy cardiovascular function.

TWO

AAM

Aam - (आम) (Mangifera indica)

Aam, also known as mango, is a fruit tree native to India. The fruit and leaves of the mango tree have been used in Ayurveda for their medicinal properties. Aam is believed to have antioxidant and anti-inflammatory properties, and it is commonly used to support healthy digestion and to treat respiratory disorders.

❧❧❧

THREE

ABHAYA

Abhaya (अभय) - (Terminalia chebula)

Abhaya is a tree native to India, and its fruit has been used in Ayurveda for centuries as a natural treatment for a variety of ailments. It is believed to have antioxidant and laxative properties, and it is commonly used to treat constipation and support healthy digestion.

ԃԃԃ

FOUR

AGARU

Agaru (अगरू) - *Aquilaria agallocha*

Agaru is a tree native to India, and its resin has been used in Ayurveda for centuries as a natural treatment for a variety of ailments. It is believed to have antiseptic and astringent properties, and it is commonly used to support healthy oral hygiene and to treat respiratory disorders.

ᐳᐳᐳ

FIVE

AJWAIN

—◌—

Ajwain - अजवाइन *(Carum Copticum)*

Ajwain, also known as Bishop's Weed, is a plant native to India, and its seeds have been used in Ayurveda for centuries as a natural treatment for a variety of ailments, including indigestion, cough, and cold. It is believed to have digestive and expectorant properties, and it is commonly used to support healthy digestion and respiratory function.

◌◌◌

SIX

AGNIMANTHA

Agnimantha (अग्नमिन्थ) - *Premna integrifolia*

Agnimantha is a tree native to India, and its bark has been used in Ayurveda for centuries as a natural treatment for a variety of ailments. It is believed to have fever-reducing and anti-inflammatory properties, and it is commonly used to treat fever and inflammation.

ᐁᐁᐁ

SEVEN

AJMODA

Ajmoda (अजमोद) - *Apium graveolens*

Ajmoda, also known as celery, is a plant native to India, and its seeds and leaves have been used in Ayurveda for centuries as a natural treatment for a variety of ailments. It is believed to have digestive and diuretic properties, and it is commonly used to support healthy digestion and to treat respiratory disorders.

EIGHT

AKARKARA

Akarkara (अकरकरा) - Anacyclus pyrethrum

Akarkara is a plant native to India, and its root has been used in Ayurveda for centuries as a natural treatment for a variety of ailments. It is believed to have digestive and expectorant properties, and it is commonly used to support healthy digestion and to treat respiratory disorders.

❧❧❧

NINE

AKASH BAIL

Akash Bail (आकाश बैल) - *Aerva lanata*

Akash Bail is a plant native to India, and its leaves have been used in Ayurveda for centuries as a natural treatment for a variety of ailments. It is believed to have diuretic and laxative properties, and it is commonly used to treat skin disorders and support healthy digestion.

TEN

AKIKA PISHTI

Akika Pishti (अककिा पष्टिटी) - Calcified Aconitum ferox

Akika pishti is a type of fine, powdery preparation made from calcified Aconitum ferox, a plant native to India. It has been used in Ayurveda for centuries as a natural treatment for a variety of ailments, including heart disorders and poor digestion. It is believed to have cardiac and digestive properties, and it is commonly used to support healthy cardiovascular function and digestion.

❧❧❧

ELEVEN

ALOE VERA

Aloe Vera (एलो वेरा) - Aloe vera

Aloe vera is a succulent plant native to Africa, and it has been used in Ayurveda for centuries as a natural treatment for a variety of ailments. It is believed to have wound-healing and anti-inflammatory properties, and it is commonly used to support healthy skin health and to treat digestive disorders.

TWELVE
AMALAKI

Amalaki (आमलकी) - *Emblica officinalis*

Amalaki, also known as Indian Gooseberry, is a tree native to India, and its fruit has been used in Ayurveda for centuries as a natural treatment for a variety of ailments. It is believed to have antioxidant and rejuvenating properties, and it is commonly used to treat anemia, support healthy skin health, and to treat a variety of ailments, including diabetes, high blood pressure, and skin disorders.

THIRTEEN

AMRITA

Amrita (अमृता) - Tinospora cordifolia

Amrita is a vine native to India, and its stem has been used in Ayurveda for centuries as a natural treatment for a variety of ailments. It is believed to have immune-boosting and fever-reducing properties, and it is commonly used to treat fever and support healthy immune function.

ppp

FOURTEEN

ARISHTA

Arishta (अरिष्ट) - *Fermented herbal decoction*

Arishta is a type of fermented herbal decoction made from a combination of herbs and plant parts. It has been used in Ayurveda for centuries as a natural treatment for a variety of ailments. It is believed to have digestive and expectorant properties, and it is commonly used to support healthy digestion and to treat respiratory disorders.

❧❧❧

FIFTEEN

ASANA

Asana (असन) - *Pterocarpus marsupium*

Asana is a tree native to India, and its bark has been used in Ayurveda for centuries as a natural treatment for a variety of ailments. It is believed to have digestive and expectorant properties, and it is commonly used to support healthy digestion and to treat respiratory disorders.

SIXTEEN
ASHOKA

Ashoka (अशोक) - *Saraca asoca*

Ashoka is a tree native to India, and its bark has been used in Ayurveda for centuries as a natural treatment for a variety of ailments. It is believed to have astringent and anti-inflammatory properties, and it is commonly used to treat menstrual disorders and support healthy digestion.

❧❧❧

SEVENTEEN
ASHWAGANDHA

Ashwagandha (अश्वगंधा) - Withania Somnifera

Ashwagandha is a plant native to India, and it has been used in Ayurveda for its medicinal properties for centuries. It is often referred to as "Indian ginseng," although it is not related to true ginseng. Ashwagandha is believed to have adaptogenic properties, meaning that it may help the body adapt to and manage stress. It is also thought to have anti-inflammatory effects and to support healthy immune system function. It is commonly used to support healthy sleep, mood, and cognitive function.

ᗡᗡᗡ

EIGHTEEN

ATIS

Atis (अतीस) - Aconitum heterophyllum

Atis is a plant native to India, and its root has been used in Ayurveda for centuries as a natural treatment for a variety of ailments. It is believed to have expectorant and digestive properties, and it is commonly used to treat respiratory disorders and support healthy digestion.

NINETEEN

BABCHI

Babchi (बाबची) - Psoralea corylifolia

Babchi is a plant native to India, and its seeds have been used in Ayurveda for centuries as a natural treatment for a variety of ailments. It is believed to have skin-healing and digestive properties, and it is commonly used to treat skin disorders and support healthy digestion.

ррр

TWENTY

BAKAYAN

Bakayan (बकायन) - *Solanum surattense*

Bakayan is a plant native to India, and its fruit has been used in Ayurveda for centuries as a natural treatment for a variety of ailments. It is believed to have digestive and expectorant properties, and it is commonly used to treat respiratory disorders and support healthy digestion.

❥❥❥

TWENTY-ONE
BAKUCHI

Bakuchi (बकुची) - Psoralea corylifolia

Bakuchi is a plant native to India, and its seeds have been used in Ayurveda for centuries as a natural treatment for a variety of ailments. It is believed to have skin-healing and digestive properties, and it is commonly used to treat skin disorders and support healthy digestion.

TWENTY-TWO
BALA (NAGABALA)

Bala (बाल) - Sida Cordifolia

Bala, (Nagabala) also known as Sida cordifolia, is a plant native to India that has been used in traditional Ayurvedic medicine for centuries. It is known for its ability to treat joint pain and improve digestion. Bala is believed to have anti-inflammatory and analgesic properties, making it useful for relieving joint pain and swelling. It is also thought to improve digestion by stimulating the production of digestive enzymes and aiding in the absorption of nutrients.

ϸϸϸ

TWENTY-THREE

BAMBOO

Bamboo (बांस) - Bambusa arundinacea

Bamboo, or Bambusa arundinacea, is a type of grass native to Asia that has been used in traditional medicine for a variety of ailments. It is believed to have medicinal properties that can help treat digestive disorders such as constipation, diarrhea, and irritable bowel syndrome. Bamboo is also thought to have anti-inflammatory and antioxidant properties, which may help to reduce inflammation in the digestive tract and improve overall gut health.

꒰ ꒰ ꒰

TWENTY-FOUR

BASANTA KUSUMAKAR

Basanta Kusumakar (बसन्त कुसुमाकर) - Michelia champaca

Basanta Kusumakar, also known as Michelia champaca, is a tropical tree native to South Asia that is known for its fragrant flowers. In traditional Ayurvedic medicine, it is used to improve digestion and treat respiratory disorders. The plant is believed to have expectorant properties, which means it can help to clear mucus from the respiratory tract and improve breathing. It is also thought to have anti-inflammatory and antioxidant properties, which may help to reduce inflammation in the respiratory system and improve overall respiratory health. In addition to its medicinal properties, the fragrant flowers of the Michelia champaca tree are often used in perfumes and as offerings in Hindu ceremonies.

ppp

TWENTY-FIVE

BHRINGARAJ

Bhringaraj (भृंगराज) - Eclipta alba

Bhringaraj, also known as Eclipta alba, is a plant native to India that has been used in traditional Ayurvedic medicine for centuries. It is known for its ability to improve hair health and treat liver disorders. Bhringaraj is believed to have rejuvenating properties that can help to strengthen and nourish the hair, promoting healthy growth and preventing hair loss. It is also thought to have liver-protective effects, making it useful for treating liver disorders and promoting overall liver health.

᎒᎒᎒

TWENTY-SIX
BHUMI AMLA

Bhumi Amla (भूमि आमला) - Phyllanthus niruri

Bhumi amla, or Phyllanthus niruri, is a plant native to India that has been used in traditional Ayurvedic medicine for a variety of ailments. It is believed to have medicinal properties that can help treat liver disorders and improve digestion. Bhumi amla is thought to have liver-protective effects, making it useful for treating liver disorders and promoting overall liver health. It is also believed to have digestive-aiding properties, which may help to improve digestion and reduce digestive complaints such as bloating and constipation.

ᐅᐅᐅ

TWENTY-SEVEN

BIBHITAKI

Bibhitaki (बिभीतकी) - Terminalia bellirica

Bibhitaki, or Terminalia bellirica, is a tree native to India that has been used in traditional Ayurvedic medicine for centuries. It is known for its ability to treat respiratory disorders and improve oral health. Bibhitaki is believed to have expectorant properties, which means it can help to clear mucus from the respiratory tract and improve breathing. It is also thought to have antimicrobial properties, making it useful for improving oral health and reducing the risk of infections in the mouth. In addition to its medicinal properties, the fruit of the Terminalia bellirica tree is often used in Ayurvedic preparations for its astringent taste.

TWENTY-EIGHT

BIMBAPHAL

Bimbaphal (बिंबाफल) - Ziziphus jujuba

Bimbaphal, also known as Ziziphus jujuba, is a plant native to India that has been used in traditional Ayurvedic medicine for centuries. It is known for its ability to treat anxiety and improve digestion. Bimbaphal is believed to have sedative properties, making it useful for reducing anxiety and promoting relaxation. It is also thought to have digestive-aiding properties, which may help to improve digestion and reduce digestive complaints such as bloating and constipation.

TWENTY-NINE
BRAHMI

Brahmi (ब्राह्मी) - Bacopa monnieri

Brahmi, or Bacopa monnieri, is a plant native to India that has been used in traditional Ayurvedic medicine for centuries. It is known for its ability to improve memory and treat anxiety and stress. Brahmi is believed to have adaptogenic properties, which means it can help the body to adapt to and cope with physical and emotional stress. It is also thought to have cognitive-enhancing effects, making it useful for improving memory and mental function.

THIRTY
CHANDAN

Chandan (चन्दन) - Santalum album

Chandan, or Santalum album, is a tree native to India that has been used in traditional Ayurvedic medicine for centuries. It is known for its ability to improve skin health and treat digestive disorders. Chandan is believed to have anti-inflammatory and antibacterial properties, making it useful for reducing inflammation in the skin and preventing the growth of bacteria. It is also thought to have digestive-aiding properties, which may help to improve digestion and reduce digestive complaints such as bloating and constipation. In addition to its medicinal properties, the essential oil extracted from the Santalum album tree is often used in perfumes and incense.

THIRTY-ONE
CHAVYA

Chavya (Piper chaba) - Hindi: Chavya

Chavya, also known as Piper chaba (English: Java Long Pepper), is a plant native to India and Southeast Asia that has been used in traditional medicine for a variety of ailments. It is known for its ability to treat indigestion, respiratory disorders, and asthma. Chavya is believed to have digestive-aiding properties, which may help to improve digestion and reduce digestive complaints such as bloating and constipation. It is also thought to have expectorant properties, which means it can help to clear mucus from the respiratory tract and improve breathing.

THIRTY-TWO
CHIRAYATA

Chirayata (चिरायता) - Swertia Chirata

Chirayata, or Swertia chirata, is a plant native to the Himalayan region of India that has been used in traditional Ayurvedic medicine for centuries. It is known for its ability to treat liver disorders and improve digestion. Chirayata is believed to have liver-protective effects, making it useful for treating liver disorders and promoting overall liver health. It is also thought to have digestive-aiding properties, which may help to improve digestion and reduce digestive complaints such as bloating and constipation.

ᗞᗞᗞ

THIRTY-THREE

CHITRAK

Chitrak (चित्रक) - *Plumbago zeylanica*

Chitrak, or Plumbago zeylanica, is a plant native to India and Sri Lanka that has been used in traditional Ayurvedic medicine for centuries. It is known for its ability to treat digestive disorders and improve appetite. Chitrak is believed to have digestive-aiding properties, which may help to improve digestion and reduce digestive complaints such as bloating and constipation. It is also thought to have appetite-stimulating effects, making it useful for improving appetite and promoting healthy weight gain. In addition to its medicinal properties, the roots of the Plumbago zeylanica plant are sometimes used as a natural dye.

THIRTY-FOUR

DALCHINI

Dalchini (दालचीनी) - Cinnamomum Zeylanicum

Dalchini, or Cinnamomum zeylanicum, is a tree native to India and Sri Lanka that is known for its aromatic bark. In traditional Ayurvedic medicine, it is used to improve digestion and treat respiratory disorders. Dalchini is believed to have digestive-aiding properties, which may help to improve digestion and reduce digestive complaints such as bloating and constipation. It is also thought to have expectorant properties, which means it can help to clear mucus from the respiratory tract and improve breathing. In addition to its medicinal properties, the bark of the Cinnamomum zeylanicum tree is commonly used as a spice in cooking.

THIRTY-FIVE

DANTI

Danti (दंती) - *Baliospermum montanum*

Danti, or Baliospermum montanum, is a plant native to India that has been used in traditional Ayurvedic medicine for centuries. It is known for its ability to improve digestion and treat respiratory disorders. Danti is believed to have digestive-aiding properties, which may help to improve digestion and reduce digestive complaints such as bloating and constipation. It is also thought to have expectorant properties, which means it can help to clear mucus from the respiratory tract and improve breathing.

❦❦❦

THIRTY-SIX

DARUHARIDRA

Daruharidra (दरुहरिद्र) - Berberis aristata

Daruharidra, or Berberis aristata, is a plant native to the Himalayan region of India that has been used in traditional Ayurvedic medicine for centuries. It is known for its ability to treat skin disorders and improve digestion. Daruharidra is believed to have anti-inflammatory and antimicrobial properties, making it useful for reducing inflammation in the skin and preventing the growth of bacteria. It is also thought to have digestive-aiding properties, which may help to improve digestion and reduce digestive complaints such as bloating and constipation. In addition to its medicinal properties, the roots of the Berberis aristata plant are sometimes used as a natural dye.

❦❦❦

THIRTY-SEVEN
DEVDARU

Devdaru (देवदारु) - Cedrus deodara

Devdaru, or Cedrus deodara, is a tree native to the Himalayan region of India that has been used in traditional Ayurvedic medicine for centuries. It is known for its ability to treat respiratory disorders and improve digestion. Devdaru is believed to have expectorant properties, which means it can help to clear mucus from the respiratory tract and improve breathing. It is also thought to have digestive-aiding properties, which may help to improve digestion and reduce digestive complaints such as bloating and constipation. In addition to its medicinal properties, the wood of the Cedrus deodara tree is commonly used in construction and carpentry.

ᘏᘏᘏ

THIRTY-EIGHT

DURALABHA

Duralabha (दुरालभा) - Fagonia Cretica

Duralabha, or Fagonia cretica, is a plant native to India and the Middle East that has been used in traditional Ayurvedic medicine for centuries. It is known for its ability to treat skin disorders and improve digestion. Duralabha is believed to have anti-inflammatory and antimicrobial properties, making it useful for reducing inflammation in the skin and preventing the growth of bacteria. It is also thought to have digestive-aiding properties, which may help to improve digestion and reduce digestive complaints such as bloating and constipation. In addition to its medicinal properties, the leaves of the Fagonia cretica plant are sometimes used as a natural dye.

THIRTY-NINE
GOKSHURA

Gokshura (गोक्षुर) - *Tribulus terrestris*

Gokshura, or Tribulus terrestris, is a plant native to India and other parts of Asia that has been used in traditional Ayurvedic medicine for centuries. It is known for its ability to treat urinary tract disorders and improve digestion. Gokshura is believed to have diuretic properties, which means it can help to increase urine production and reduce water retention in the body. It is also thought to have digestive-aiding properties, which may help to improve digestion and reduce digestive complaints such as bloating and constipation.

ᐁᐁᐁ

FORTY

GUDUCHI

Guduchi (गुडूची) - Tinospora cordifolia

Guduchi, or Tinospora cordifolia, is a plant native to India that has been used in traditional Ayurvedic medicine for centuries. It is known for its ability to treat fever, inflammation, and liver disorders. Guduchi is believed to have immune-boosting properties, making it useful for reducing inflammation and fighting infections. It is also thought to have liver-protective effects, making it useful for treating liver disorders and promoting overall liver health.

ᗞᗞᗞ

FORTY-ONE

GUGGULU

Guggulu (गुग्गुलु) - Commiphora mukul

Guggulu, or Commiphora mukul, is a tree native to India and the Middle East that has been used in traditional Ayurvedic medicine for centuries. It is known for its ability to treat joint pain and improve metabolism. Guggulu is believed to have anti-inflammatory and analgesic properties, making it useful for relieving joint pain and swelling. It is also thought to have metabolism-boosting effects, which may help to improve weight management and support healthy body composition. In addition to its medicinal properties, the resin extracted from the Commiphora mukul tree is sometimes used as a natural incense.

FORTY-TWO
GURMAR

Gurmar (गुरुमर) - Gymnema sylvestre

Gurmar, or Gymnema sylvestre, is a plant native to India that has been used in traditional Ayurvedic medicine for centuries. It is known for its ability to treat diabetes and improve digestion. Gurmar is believed to have blood sugar-lowering effects, making it useful for managing diabetes and regulating blood sugar levels. It is also thought to have digestive-aiding properties, which may help to improve digestion and reduce digestive complaints such as bloating and constipation.

FORTY-THREE

HARIDRA

Haridra (हरिद्र) - Curcuma longa

Haridra, or Curcuma longa, is a plant native to India that has been used in traditional Ayurvedic medicine for centuries. It is known for its ability to improve skin health and treat digestive disorders. Haridra is believed to have anti-inflammatory and antioxidant properties, making it useful for reducing inflammation in the skin and preventing oxidative damage. It is also thought to have digestive-aiding properties, which may help to improve digestion and reduce digestive complaints such as bloating and constipation. In addition to its medicinal properties, the rhizomes of the Curcuma longa plant are commonly used as a spice in cooking.

FORTY-FOUR
HARITAKI

Haritaki (हरीतकी) - Terminalia Chebula

Haritaki, or Terminalia chebula, is a tree native to India and other parts of Asia that has been used in traditional Ayurvedic medicine for centuries. It is known for its ability to treat constipation and improve digestion. Haritaki is believed to have laxative properties, which means it can help to relieve constipation and promote regular bowel movements. It is also thought to have digestive-aiding properties, which may help to improve digestion and reduce digestive complaints such as bloating and constipation. In addition to its medicinal properties, the fruit of the Terminalia chebula tree is often used in Ayurvedic preparations for its astringent taste.

 PPP

FORTY-FIVE
INDRAVARUNI

Indravaruni (इन्द्रवरुनी) - Citrullus colocynthis

Indravaruni, or Citrullus colocynthis, is a plant native to India and other parts of Asia that has been used in traditional Ayurvedic medicine for centuries. It is known for its ability to treat constipation and improve digestion. Indravaruni is believed to have laxative properties, which means it can help to relieve constipation and promote regular bowel movements. It is also thought to have digestive-aiding properties, which may help to improve digestion and reduce digestive complaints such as bloating and constipation.

ϷϷϷ

FORTY-SIX

JAMBU

Jambu (जम्बू) - Syzygium cumini

Jambu, or Syzygium cumini, is a tree native to India and other parts of Asia that has been used in traditional Ayurvedic medicine for centuries. It is known for its ability to improve digestion and treat respiratory disorders. Jambu is believed to have digestive-aiding properties, which may help to improve digestion and reduce digestive complaints such as bloating and constipation. It is also thought to have expectorant properties, which means it can help to clear mucus from the respiratory tract and improve breathing. In addition to its medicinal properties, the fruit of the Syzygium cumini tree is commonly eaten as a snack or used to make jams and jellies.

ϐϐϐ

FORTY-SEVEN
JIVANTI

*Jivanti (जीवान्ती) - **Leptadenia reticulata***

Jivanti, or Leptadenia reticulata, is a plant native to India that has been used in traditional Ayurvedic medicine for centuries. It is known for its ability to improve immune function and treat respiratory disorders. Jivanti is believed to have immune-boosting properties, making it useful for supporting the body's natural defenses and protecting against infections. It is also thought to have expectorant properties, which means it can help to clear mucus from the respiratory tract and improve breathing.

FORTY-EIGHT

JYOTISHMATI

Jyotishmati (ज्योतिष्मती) - Celastrus paniculatus

Jyotishmati, or Celastrus paniculatus, is a plant native to India that has been used in traditional Ayurvedic medicine for centuries. It is known for its ability to improve memory and treat anxiety and stress. Jyotishmati is believed to have cognitive-enhancing effects, making it useful for improving memory and focus. It is also thought to have anxiolytic properties, which means it can help to reduce anxiety and promote relaxation.

FORTY-NINE
KACHNAR

Kachnar (कचनार) - *Bauhinia variegata*

Kachnar, or Bauhinia variegata, is a tree native to India and other parts of Asia that has been used in traditional Ayurvedic medicine for centuries. It is known for its ability to treat respiratory disorders and improve skin health. Kachnar is believed to have expectorant properties, which means it can help to clear mucus from the respiratory tract and improve breathing. It is also thought to have anti-inflammatory and antimicrobial properties, making it useful for reducing inflammation in the skin and preventing the growth of bacteria. In addition to its medicinal properties, the flowers of the Bauhinia variegata tree are often used in Ayurvedic preparations for their astringent taste.

❧❧❧

FIFTY
KACHUR

Kachur (कचूर) - *Curcuma zedoaria*

Kachur, or Curcuma zedoaria, is a plant native to India and other parts of Asia that has been used in traditional Ayurvedic medicine for centuries. It is known for its ability to treat digestive disorders and improve skin health. Kachur is believed to have digestive-aiding properties, which may help to improve digestion and reduce digestive complaints such as bloating and constipation. It is also thought to have anti-inflammatory and antimicrobial properties, making it useful for reducing inflammation in the skin and preventing the growth of bacteria. In addition to its medicinal properties, the rhizomes of the Curcuma zedoaria plant are commonly used as a spice in cooking.

❦❦❦

FIFTY-ONE
KAIDARYA

Kaidarya (कदैरया) - Cichorium Itybus

Kaidarya, or Cichorium intybus, is a plant native to Europe and Asia that has been used in traditional Ayurvedic medicine for centuries. It is known for its ability to treat digestive disorders and improve liver function. Kaidarya is believed to have digestive-aiding properties, which may help to improve digestion and reduce digestive complaints such as bloating and constipation. It is also thought to have liver-protective effects, making it useful for treating liver disorders and promoting overall liver health. In addition to its medicinal properties, the leaves of the Cichorium intybus plant are sometimes used as a natural dye.

ᳬᳬᳬ

FIFTY-TWO
KAKOLI

Kakoli (काकोली) - Fritillaria roylei

Kakoli, or Fritillaria roylei, is a plant native to the Himalayan region of India that has been used in traditional Ayurvedic medicine for centuries. It is known for its ability to improve digestion and treat respiratory disorders. Kakoli is believed to have digestive-aiding properties, which may help to improve digestion and reduce digestive complaints such as bloating and constipation. It is also thought to have expectorant properties, which means it can help to clear mucus from the respiratory tract and improve breathing. In addition to its medicinal properties, the bulbs of the Fritillaria roylei plant are sometimes used as a natural dye.

FIFTY-THREE

KAKU

Kaku (काकू) - Ficus Lacor

Kaku, or Ficus Lacor, is a tree native to India and other parts of Asia that has been used in traditional Ayurvedic medicine for centuries. It is known for its ability to improve digestion and treat respiratory disorders. Kaku is believed to have digestive-aiding properties, which may help to improve digestion and reduce digestive complaints such as bloating and constipation. It is also thought to have expectorant properties, which means it can help to clear mucus from the respiratory tract and improve breathing. In addition to its medicinal properties, the latex of the Ficus lacor tree is sometimes used as a natural rubber.

ϸϸϸ

FIFTY-FOUR

KAMAL

Kamal (कमल) - Nelumbo Nucifera

Kamal, or Nelumbo nucifera, is a water plant native to India and other parts of Asia that has been used in traditional Ayurvedic medicine for centuries. It is known for its ability to treat respiratory disorders and improve digestion. Kamal is believed to have expectorant properties, which means it can help to clear mucus from the respiratory tract and improve breathing. It is also thought to have digestive-aiding properties, which may help to improve digestion and reduce digestive complaints such as bloating and constipation. In addition to its medicinal properties, the flowers of the Nelumbo nucifera plant are often used in Ayurvedic preparations for their astringent taste.

FIFTY-FIVE

KAMAL KESAR

Kamal Kesar (कमल केसर) - Nelumbo nucifera

Kamal Kesar, or Nelumbo nucifera, is a water plant native to India and other parts of Asia that has been used in traditional Ayurvedic medicine for centuries. It is known for its ability to improve skin health and treat digestive disorders. Kamal Kesar is believed to have anti-inflammatory and antioxidant properties, making it useful for reducing inflammation in the skin and preventing oxidative damage. It is also thought to have digestive-aiding properties, which may help to improve digestion and reduce digestive complaints such as bloating and constipation. In addition to its medicinal properties, the flowers of the Nelumbo nucifera plant are often used in Ayurvedic preparations for their astringent taste.

❧❧❧

FIFTY-SIX
KANCHANAR

Kanchanar (कंचनार) - Bauhinia variegata

Kanchanar, or Bauhinia variegata, is a tree native to India and other parts of Asia that has been used in traditional Ayurvedic medicine for centuries. It is known for its ability to treat thyroid disorders and improve digestion. Kanchanar is believed to have thyroid-regulating effects, making it useful for treating thyroid disorders and balancing thyroid hormone levels. It is also thought to have digestive-aiding properties, which may help to improve digestion and reduce digestive complaints such as bloating and constipation. In addition to its medicinal properties, the flowers of the Bauhinia variegata tree are often used in Ayurvedic preparations for their astringent taste.

ᴘᴘᴘ

FIFTY-SEVEN

KANKUSTA

Kankusta (कंकूसृता) - *Gymnema sylvestre*

Kankusta, or Gymnema sylvestre, is a plant native to India that has been used in traditional Ayurvedic medicine for centuries. It is known for its ability to treat diabetes and improve digestion. Kankusta is believed to have blood sugar-lowering effects, making it useful for managing diabetes and regulating blood sugar levels. It is also thought to have digestive-aiding properties, which may help to improve digestion and reduce digestive complaints such as bloating and constipation.

❧❧❧

FIFTY-EIGHT
KANTAKARI

Kantakari (कंटकारी) (Solanum xanthocarpum)

Kantakari (English: Yellow Berried Nightshade) or Solanum Xanthocarpum, is a plant native to India that has been used in traditional Ayurvedic medicine for centuries. It is known for its ability to treat a variety of ailments, including asthma, cough, and cold. Kantakari is believed to have expectorant properties, which means it can help to clear mucus from the respiratory tract and improve breathing. It is also thought to have anti-inflammatory and antimicrobial properties, making it useful for reducing inflammation in the respiratory tract and preventing the growth of bacteria.

ᐯᐯᐯ

FIFTY-NINE

KARAVELLAKA

Karavellaka (करवेल्लक) - *Carum roxburghianum*

Karavellaka, or Carum roxburghianum, is a plant native to India that has been used in traditional Ayurvedic medicine for centuries. It is known for its ability to improve digestion and treat respiratory disorders. Karavellaka is believed to have digestive-aiding properties, which may help to improve digestion and reduce digestive complaints such as bloating and constipation. It is also thought to have expectorant properties, which means it can help to clear mucus from the respiratory tract and improve breathing. In addition to its medicinal properties, the seeds of the Carum roxburghianum plant are often used as a spice in cooking.

❧❧❧

SIXTY

KARKATSHRINGI

Karkatshringi (कर्कटश्रृंगी) - Paederia Foetida

Karkatshringi, or Paederia foetida, is a plant native to India that has been used in traditional Ayurvedic medicine for centuries. It is known for its ability to treat joint pain and improve digestion. Karkatshringi is believed to have anti-inflammatory and analgesic properties, making it useful for reducing inflammation in the joints and relieving pain. It is also thought to have digestive-aiding properties, which may help to improve digestion and reduce digestive complaints such as bloating and constipation.

SIXTY-ONE
KARONDA

Karonda (करौंदा) - Carissa Carandas

Karonda, or Carissa carandas, is a plant native to India that has been used in traditional Ayurvedic medicine for centuries. It is known for its ability to treat digestive disorders and improve skin health. Karonda is believed to have digestive-aiding properties, which may help to improve digestion and reduce digestive complaints such as bloating and constipation. It is also thought to have anti-inflammatory and antimicrobial properties, making it useful for reducing inflammation in the skin and preventing the growth of bacteria. In addition to its medicinal properties, the fruit of the Carissa carandas plant is sometimes used as a natural dye.

ᗡᗡᗡ

SIXTY-TWO
KARPOOR

Karpoor (करपूर) - Cinnamomum Camphora

Karpoor, or Cinnamomum camphora, is a tree native to India and other parts of Asia that has been used in traditional Ayurvedic medicine for centuries. It is known for its ability to improve digestion and treat respiratory disorders. Karpoor is believed to have digestive-aiding properties, which may help to improve digestion and reduce digestive complaints such as bloating and constipation. It is also thought to have expectorant properties, which means it can help to clear mucus from the respiratory tract and improve breathing. In addition to its medicinal properties, the essential oil of the Cinnamomum camphora tree is often used in aromatherapy.

SIXTY-THREE

KAUNCH

Kaunch (कौंच) - Mucuna Pruriens

Kaunch, or Mucuna pruriens, is a plant native to India and other parts of Asia that has been used in traditional Ayurvedic medicine for centuries. It is known for its ability to improve sperm count and treat Parkinson's disease. Kaunch is believed to have aphrodisiac properties, which may help to improve sexual function and increase sperm count. It is also thought to have neuroprotective effects, making it useful for treating Parkinson's disease and other neurological disorders

♡♡♡

SIXTY-FOUR

KESAR

Kesar (कसर) - Crocus Sativus

Kesar, or Crocus Sativus, is a plant native to India and other parts of Asia that has been used in traditional Ayurvedic medicine for centuries. It is known for its ability to improve skin health and treat digestive disorders. Kesar is believed to have antioxidant and anti-inflammatory properties, making it useful for protecting the skin from damage and reducing inflammation in the digestive system. It is also thought to have digestive-aiding properties, which may help to improve digestion and reduce digestive complaints such as bloating and constipation.

❦❦❦

SIXTY-FIVE

KHURASANI AJWAIN

Khurasani ajwain (खुरासानी अजवाइन) - Hyoscyamus Niger

Khurasani ajwain, or Hyoscyamus niger, is a plant native to India and other parts of Asia that has been used in traditional Ayurvedic medicine for centuries. It is known for its ability to treat digestive disorders and improve oral health. Khurasani ajwain is believed to have digestive-aiding properties, which may help to improve digestion and reduce digestive complaints such as bloating and constipation. It is also thought to have antispasmodic and analgesic properties, making it useful for relieving pain and reducing muscle spasms in the digestive system. In addition to its medicinal properties, the seeds of the Hyoscyamus niger plant are sometimes used as *a spice in cooking.*

❧❧❧

SIXTY-SIX
KOKILAKSHA

Kokilaksha (कोकलिाक्ष) - *Asteracantha Longifolia*

Kokilaksha, or Asteracantha longifolia, is a plant native to India that has been used in traditional Ayurvedic medicine for centuries. It is known for its ability to treat urinary tract disorders and improve digestion. Kokilaksha is believed to have diuretic properties, which means it can help to increase urine production and flush out toxins from the body. It is also thought to have digestive-aiding properties, which may help to improve digestion and reduce digestive complaints such as bloating and constipation. In addition to its medicinal properties, the seeds of the Asteracantha longifolia plant are sometimes used as a spice in cooking.

ᚦᚦᚦ

SIXTY-SEVEN

KUDA

Kuda (कुड़ा) - Holarrhena Antidysenterica

Kuda, or Holarrhena antidysenterica, is a plant native to India and other parts of Asia that has been used in traditional Ayurvedic medicine for centuries. It is known for its ability to treat digestive disorders and improve skin health. Kuda is believed to have digestive-aiding properties, which may help to improve digestion and reduce digestive complaints such as bloating and constipation. It is also thought to have anti-inflammatory and antimicrobial properties, making it useful for reducing inflammation in the digestive system and preventing the growth of bacteria.

♥♥♥

SIXTY-EIGHT

KUDZU

Kudzu (कुड्ज़ू) - Pueraria Lobata

Kudzu, or Pueraria lobata, is a plant native to Asia that has been used in traditional Chinese medicine for centuries. It is known for its ability to treat alcoholism and improve digestion. Kudzu is believed to have anti-alcoholic properties, which may help to reduce the craving for alcohol and prevent relapse in those recovering from addiction. It is also thought to have digestive-aiding properties, which may help to improve digestion and reduce digestive complaints such as bloating and constipation.

SIXTY-NINE

KUSHTHA

Kushtha (कुष्ठ) - Saussurea Lappa

Kushtha, or Saussurea lappa, is a plant native to the Himalayan region of India that has been used in traditional Ayurvedic medicine for centuries. It is known for its ability to treat skin disorders and improve blood circulation. Kushtha is believed to have skin-protective and blood-purifying properties, making it useful for protecting the skin from damage and improving the quality of the blood. It is also thought to have anti-inflammatory and antimicrobial properties, which may help to reduce inflammation in the skin and prevent the growth of bacteria. It is also believed to improve blood circulation and reduce inflammation. Saussurea lappa, also known as Kushtha, is a perennial herb with long, narrow leaves and small white flowers. The roots of the plant are used medicinally, and are often dried and powdered for use in capsules or as a decoction.

❦❦❦

SEVENTY

KUTAJA

Kutaja (कुटज) - Holarrhena Antidysenterica

Kutaja is a small shrub native to India and other parts of South Asia. It has been used in Ayurvedic medicine for centuries to treat digestive disorders, such as diarrhea and dysentery. It is also believed to improve skin health and reduce inflammation. Holarrhena antidysenterica, also known as Kutaja, is a small shrub with yellow or orange flowers and small, dark-colored fruits. The bark and seeds of the plant are used medicinally, and are often ground into a powder or made into an extract for use in capsules or as a decoction.

ᗡᗡᗡ

SEVENTY-ONE
KUTKI

Kutki (कुटकी) - Picrorhiza Hurroa

Kutki is a medicinal plant native to the Himalayan region of India. It has been used in Ayurvedic medicine for centuries to treat liver disorders and improve digestion. It is also believed to have anti-inflammatory and antioxidant properties.

Picrorhiza kurroa, also known as Kutki, is a small, perennial herb with dark green leaves and small purple flowers. The roots of the plant are used medicinally, and are often dried and powdered for use in capsules or as a decoction. The medicinal properties of Kutki are believed to be due to the presence of a number of active compounds, including picroside-I, picroside-II, and kutkin. These compounds are thought to *have liver-protective, anti-inflammatory, and antioxidant effects.In Ayurvedic medicine, Kutki is typically used in the form of a decoction or capsule. It is usually taken orally, and is believed to be most effective when taken on an empty stomach. It is generally considered to be safe when taken in recommended doses, although it may cause digestive upset in some people.*

ϦϦϦ

SEVENTY-TWO
LAKSHMANA

Lakshmana (लक्ष्मण) - Selaginella Bryopteris

Lakshmana, or Selaginella bryopteris, is a plant native to India and other parts of Asia that has been used in traditional Ayurvedic medicine for centuries. It is known for its ability to improve digestion and treat respiratory disorders. Lakshmana is believed to have digestive-aiding properties, which may help to improve digestion and reduce digestive complaints such as bloating and constipation. It is also thought to have expectorant properties, which means it can help to clear mucus from the respiratory tract and improve breathing.

ÞÞÞ

SEVENTY-THREE

LODHRA

Lodhra (लोधरा) - *Symplocos Racemosa*

Lodhra, or Symplocos racemosa, is a plant native to India and other parts of Asia that has been used in traditional Ayurvedic medicine for centuries. It is known for its ability to improve skin health and treat menstrual disorders. Lodhra is believed to have skin-protective and astringent properties, making it useful for protecting the skin from damage and reducing the secretion of fluids from the skin. It is also thought to have uterine-toning properties, which may help to regulate the menstrual cycle and reduce menstrual complaints such as cramps and heavy bleeding.

SEVENTY-FOUR
MADAYANTIKA

Madayantika (मादयतंकिा) - Marsdenia Tenacissima

Madayantika, or Marsdenia tenacissima, is a plant native to India and other parts of Asia that has been used in traditional Ayurvedic medicine for centuries. It is known for its ability to treat digestive disorders and improve skin health. Madayantika is believed to have digestive-aiding properties, which may help to improve digestion and reduce digestive complaints such as bloating and constipation. It is also thought to have skin-protective and astringent properties, making it useful for protecting the skin from damage and reducing the secretion of fluids from the skin.

ᘖᘖᘖ

SEVENTY-FIVE
MADHUKA

Madhuka (माधूक) - Madhuca Latifolia

Madhuka, or Madhuca latifolia, is a tree native to India and other parts of Asia that has been used in traditional Ayurvedic medicine for centuries. It is known for its ability to improve digestion and treat respiratory disorders. Madhuka is believed to have digestive-aiding properties, which may help to improve digestion and reduce digestive complaints such as bloating and constipation. It is also thought to have expectorant properties, which means it can help to clear mucus from the respiratory tract and improve breathing.

SEVENTY-SIX
MADHUVANTI

Madhuvanti (मध्वन्ती) - Madhuca Longifolia

Madhuvanti, or Madhuca longifolia, is a tree native to India and other parts of Asia that has been used in traditional Ayurvedic medicine for centuries. It is known for its ability to improve skin health and treat digestive disorders. Madhuvanti is believed to have skin-protective and astringent properties, making it useful for protecting the skin from damage and reducing the secretion of fluids from the skin. It is also thought to have digestive-aiding properties, which may help to improve digestion and reduce digestive complaints such as bloating and constipation

SEVENTY-SEVEN
MAHANIMBA

Mahanimba (महानिम्बा) - Melia Azadirachta

Mahanimba, or Melia azadirachta, is a tree native to India and other parts of Asia that has been used in traditional Ayurvedic medicine for centuries. It is known for its ability to treat fever and improve skin health. Mahanimba is believed to have fever-reducing and skin-protective properties, making it useful for reducing fever and protecting the skin from damage. It is also thought to have antimicrobial properties, which may help to prevent the growth of bacteria.

❧❧❧

SEVENTY-EIGHT
MANJISTHA

Manjistha (मंजिष्ठा) - Rubia Cordifolia

Manjistha is a medicinal plant native to India and other parts of South Asia. It has been used in Ayurvedic medicine for centuries to improve blood circulation and treat a variety of skin disorders. Rubia cordifolia, also known as Manjistha, is a perennial climbing plant with small, red flowers and thin, delicate stems. The roots of the plant are used medicinally, and are often dried and powdered for use in capsules or as a decoction.

SEVENTY-NINE

MARICHA

Maricha (Piper nigrum)

Maricha (Piper nigrum) also known as Kalimirch in Hindi and Black Pepper in English, is a popular spice native to India and other parts of South Asia. It has been used in Ayurvedic medicine for centuries to treat a variety of ailments, including indigestion, cough, and cold. Black pepper is a small, flowering vine with small, green berries that turn black when they are fully ripe. The dried, ground berries are used as a spice, while the whole berries can be used medicinally. The medicinal properties of black pepper are believed to be due to the presence of a number of active compounds, including piperine, which is thought to have anti-inflammatory and antioxidant effects.In Ayurvedic medicine, black pepper is often used in the form of a decoction or infusion. It is usually taken orally, and is believed to be most effective when taken on an empty stomach.

❦❦❦

EIGHTY
MASHAPARNI

Mashaparni (मशापर्णी) - Teramnus Labialis

Mashaparni (Teramnus labialis) is a medicinal plant used in Ayurveda, the traditional medical system of India. It is native to the Indian subcontinent and is also found in parts of Southeast Asia. Mashaparni is known for its ability to improve memory and treat anxiety and stress. It is often used in the form of a powder or decoction. In terms of its physical use, Mashaparni is believed to improve cognitive function and memory retention. It is also used to treat anxiety and stress, as it is thought to have a calming effect on the mind and body. In addition to its use as a medicinal herb, Mashaparni is also used in traditional Ayurvedic beauty treatments for its skin-nourishing properties. Mashaparni is believed to contain compounds such as flavonoids and alkaloids, which are thought to have antioxidant and anti-inflammatory effects

❧❧❧

EIGHTY-ONE

METHI

Methi (मेथी) - Trigonella Foenum-Graecum

Methi (Trigonella foenum-graecum) is another medicinal plant used in Ayurveda. It is native to the Mediterranean region and is now widely cultivated in many parts of the world. Methi is commonly used to improve digestion and treat respiratory disorders. It is often used in the form of a powder or decoction, or the seeds may be roasted and consumed as a spice. In terms of its physical use, Methi is believed to stimulate digestion and improve the absorption of nutrients. It is also used to treat respiratory disorders such as asthma and bronchitis, as it is thought to have expectorant and decongestant properties. In addition to its medicinal uses, Methi is also used as a spice in cooking and is believed to have antioxidant and anti-inflammatory properties. Methi is believed to *contain compounds such as saponins and mucilage, which are thought to have expectorant and demulcent properties.*

❧❧❧

EIGHTY-TWO

MUSTAK

Mustak (मुस्तक) - Cyperus rotundus

Mustak (Cyperus rotundus) is another medicinal plant used in Ayurveda. It is native to India and is also found in other parts of Asia, Africa, and Europe. Mustak is commonly used to treat digestive disorders and improve oral health. It is often used in the form of a powder or decoction, or the roots may be chewed or used as a mouth rinse.In terms of its physical use, Mustak is believed to stimulate digestion and improve the absorption of nutrients. It is also used to treat digestive disorders such as constipation and indigestion. In addition to its medicinal uses, Mustak is also used in traditional Ayurvedic beauty treatments for its skin-nourishing properties. Mustak is believed to contain compounds such as essential oils and *tannins, which are thought to have astringent and antioxidant effects.*

❤❤❤

EIGHTY-THREE
NAGARA

Nagara (नगर) - Zingiber Officinale

Nagara (Zingiber officinale) is another medicinal plant used in Ayurveda. It is native to South Asia and is now widely cultivated in many parts of the world. Nagara is commonly used to treat digestive disorders and improve skin health. It is often used in the form of a powder or decoction, or the roots may be used fresh or dried as a spice in cooking. In terms of its physical use, Nagara is believed to stimulate digestion and improve the absorption of nutrients. It is also used to treat digestive disorders such as indigestion and bloating. In addition to its medicinal uses, Nagara is also used in traditional Ayurvedic beauty treatments for its skin-nourishing properties. It is believed to have antioxidant and anti-inflammatory properties, which may help to improve the appearance of the skin.

❦❦❦

EIGHTY-FOUR
NAGKESAR

Nagkesar (नागकेसर) - Mesua Ferrea

Nagkesar (Mesua ferrea) is another medicinal plant used in Ayurveda. It is native to India and is also found in other parts of Asia. Nagkesar is commonly used to improve digestion and treat respiratory disorders. It is often used in the form of a powder or decoction, or the flowers may be used fresh or dried as a fragrant addition to traditional Ayurvedic incense and perfumes. In terms of its physical use, Nagkesar is believed to stimulate digestion and improve the absorption of nutrients. It is also used to treat respiratory disorders such as asthma and bronchitis, as it is thought to have expectorant properties. In addition to its medicinal uses, Nagkesar is also used in traditional Ayurvedic beauty treatments for its skin-nourishing properties. It is believed to have antioxidant and anti-

inflammatory properties, which may help to improve the appearance of the skin.

❧❧❧

EIGHTY-FIVE

NEEM

Neem (नीम) - Azadirachta Indica

Neem (Azadirachta Indica) is a medicinal plant used in Ayurveda, the traditional medical system of India. It is native to the Indian subcontinent and is also found in parts of Southeast Asia. Neem is commonly used to treat skin disorders and improve oral health. It is often used in the form of a powder or decoction.. In terms of its physical use, Neem is believed to have anti-inflammatory and antibacterial properties and is therefore often used to treat skin disorders such as acne and eczema.

It is also believed to improve oral health by reducing plaque and preventing the build-up of bacteria in the mouth. In addition to its medicinal uses, Neem is also used in traditional Ayurvedic beauty treatments for its skin-

nourishing properties.

❦❦❦

EIGHTY-SIX
NILOTPALA

Nilotpala (नीलोत्पल) - Nymphaea stellata

Nilotpala (Nymphaea stellata) is another medicinal plant used in Ayurveda. It is native to the Indian subcontinent and is also found in other parts of Asia. Nilotpala is commonly used to treat digestive disorders and improve skin health. It is often used in the form of a powder or decoction.In terms of its physical use, Nilotpala is believed to stimulate digestion and improve the absorption of nutrients. It is also used to treat digestive disorders such as indigestion and bloating. In addition to its medicinal uses, Nilotpala is also used in traditional Ayurvedic beauty treatments for its skin-nourishing properties. It is believed to have antioxidant and anti-inflammatory properties, which may help to improve the appearance of the skin.

DR. JAGADEESH PILLAI

❧❧❧

EIGHTY-SEVEN
PADMAKA

Padmaka (पद्मक) - Prunus Cerasoides

Padmaka (Prunus cerasoides) is another medicinal plant used in Ayurveda. It is native to the Himalayan region of India and is also found in other parts of Asia. Padmaka is commonly used to improve digestion and treat respiratory disorders. It is often used in the form of a powder or decoction.In terms of its physical use, Padmaka is believed to stimulate digestion and improve the absorption of nutrients. It is also used to treat respiratory disorders such as asthma and bronchitis, as it is thought to have expectorant properties. In addition to its medicinal uses, Padmaka is also used in traditional Ayurvedic beauty treatments for its skin-nourishing properties. It is believed to have antioxidant and anti-inflammatory properties, which may help to improve the appearance of *the skin.*

❥❥❥

EIGHTY-EIGHT
PARNAYA

Parnaya (परनाया) - Fumaria officinalis

Parnaya (Fumaria officinalis) is a small annual herb that is native to Europe and Asia. It has been used in traditional Ayurvedic medicine for centuries to treat various skin disorders and improve digestion.The chemical properties of Parnaya include the presence of alkaloids, flavonoids, and saponins. These compounds are thought to contribute to the herb's medicinal effects. In terms of physical and psychological use, Parnaya is often taken orally as a digestive aid or applied topically to the skin to treat various disorders. It is also believed to have mild sedative effects and may be used to promote relaxation and reduce anxiety. Other potential benefits of Parnaya include its ability to reduce inflammation, improve immune function, and protect against oxidative stress. It may also have antioxidant and anticancer properties.

❥❥❥

EIGHTY-NINE
PATOL

Patol (पतोल) - *Trichosanthes Dioica*

Patol (Trichosanthes dioica) is a climbing vine that is native to Asia. It has been used in traditional Ayurvedic medicine for its medicinal properties, including its ability to improve digestion and oral health. The chemical properties of Patol include the presence of trichosanthin, a protein-bound polysaccharide that is thought to contribute to the herb's medicinal effects. In terms of physical and psychological use, Patol is typically taken orally as a digestive aid or applied topically to the skin to treat various disorders. It is also believed to have mild sedative effects and may be used to promote relaxation and reduce anxiety. Other potential benefits of Patol include its ability to reduce inflammation, improve immune function, and protect against oxidative stress.

It may also have anticancer and antiviral properties.

❧❧❧

NINETY
PIPPALI

Pippali (पिप्पली) - Piper Longum

Pippali (Piper longum) is a perennial vine that is native to the tropics of Asia. It has been used in traditional Ayurvedic medicine for centuries to treat respiratory disorders and improve digestion.The chemical properties of Pippali include the presence of piperine, a compound that is thought to contribute to the herb's medicinal effects.In terms of physical and psychological use, Pippali is often taken orally as a digestive aid or applied topically to the skin to treat various disorders. It is also believed to have mild stimulant effects and may be used to improve energy and mental clarity.Other potential benefits of Pippali include its ability to reduce inflammation, improve immune function, and protect against oxidative stress. It may also have antioxidant, anticancer, and antiviral properties.

NINETY-ONE
PIPPALIMULA

Pippalimula (Piper Longum root) - Hindi: Pipali Mool

Pippalimula (Piper longum root) is the root of the Piper longum plant, which is native to the tropics of Asia. It has been used in traditional Ayurvedic medicine for centuries to treat a variety of ailments, including indigestion, respiratory disorders, and asthma.The chemical properties of Pippalimula include the presence of piperine, a compound that is thought to contribute to the herb's medicinal effects. In terms of physical and psychological use, Pippalimula is often taken orally as a digestive aid or applied topically to the skin to treat various disorders. It is also believed to have mild stimulant effects and may be used to improve energy and mental clarity.Other potential benefits of Pippalimula include its ability to reduce inflammation, improve immune function, and protect against oxidative stress.

It may also have antioxidant, anticancer, and antiviral properties.

ϸϸϸ

NINETY-TWO
PRASARINI

Prasarini (पुरसरणी) - Paederia foetida

Prasarini (Paederia foetida) is a perennial herb that is native to Asia. It has been used in traditional Ayurvedic medicine for its medicinal properties, including its ability to treat joint pain and improve digestion. The chemical properties of Prasarini include the presence of flavonoids, saponins, and tannins. These compounds are thought to contribute to the herb's medicinal effects. In terms of physical and psychological use, Prasarini is typically taken orally as a digestive aid or applied topically to the skin to treat various disorders. It is also believed to have mild sedative effects and may be used to promote relaxation and reduce anxiety. Other potential benefits of Prasarini include its ability to reduce inflammation, improve immune function, and protect against *oxidative stress. It may also have antioxidant, anticancer, and antiviral properties.*

ᏚᏙᏚ

NINETY-THREE

PRISHNIPARNI

Prishniparni (पृष्णीपर्णी) - Uraria Picta

Prishniparni (Uraria picta) is a perennial herb that is native to Asia. It has been used in traditional Ayurvedic medicine for its medicinal properties, including its ability to improve urinary health and treat digestive disorders. The chemical properties of Prishniparni include the presence of flavonoids, saponins, and tannins. These compounds are thought to contribute to the herb's medicinal effects. In terms of physical and psychological use, Prishniparni is typically taken orally as a digestive aid or applied topically to the skin to treat various disorders. It is also believed to have mild sedative effects and may be used to promote relaxation and reduce anxiety. Other potential benefits of Prishniparni include its ability to reduce inflammation, improve immune function, and protect against oxidative stress. It may also have antioxidant, anticancer, and antiviral properties.

❦❦❦

NINETY-FOUR

PUNARNAVA

Punarnava (पुनर्नवा) - Boerhavia Diffusa

Punarnava (Boerhavia diffusa) is a perennial herb that is native to Asia and the Americas. It has been used in traditional Ayurvedic medicine for its medicinal properties, including its ability to treat edema and improve liver function. The chemical properties of Punarnava include the presence of flavonoids, saponins, and tannins. These compounds are thought to contribute to the herb's medicinal effects. In terms of physical and psychological use, Punarnava is typically taken orally as a digestive aid or applied topically to the skin to treat various disorders. It is also believed to have mild sedative effects and may be used to promote relaxation and reduce anxiety. Other potential benefits of Punarnava include its ability to reduce inflammation, improve immune function, and protect against oxidative stress. It may also have antioxidant, anticancer, and antiviral properties.

❦❦❦

NINETY-FIVE

RASNA

Rasna (रसूना) - Pluchea Lanceolata

Rasna (Pluchea lanceolata) is a perennial herb that is native to Asia. It has been used in traditional Ayurvedic medicine for its medicinal properties, including its ability to treat joint pain and improve digestion. The chemical properties of Rasna include the presence of flavonoids, saponins, and tannins. These compounds are thought to contribute to the herb's medicinal effects. In terms of physical and psychological use, Rasna is typically taken orally as a digestive aid or applied topically to the skin to treat various disorders. It is also believed to have mild sedative effects and may be used to promote relaxation and reduce anxiety. Other potential benefits of Rasna include its ability to reduce inflammation, *improve immune function, and protect against oxidative stress. It may also have antioxidant, anticancer, and antiviral properties.*

ᐅᐅᐅ

NINETY-SIX
SAHACHARA

Sahachara (सहचर) - Strobilanthes Ciliatus

Sahachara (Strobilanthes ciliatus) is a medicinal plant used in Ayurveda, the traditional medical system of India. It is native to the Indian subcontinent and is also found in other parts of Asia. Sahachara is commonly used to treat respiratory disorders and improve digestion. It is often used in the form of a powder or decoction. In terms of its physical use, Sahachara is believed to have expectorant properties and is therefore often used to treat respiratory disorders such as asthma and bronchitis. It is also believed to stimulate digestion and improve the absorption of nutrients.

❦❦❦

NINETY-SEVEN
SAPTAPARNA

Saptaparna (सप्तपर्ण) - Alstonia Scholaris

Saptaparna (Alstonia scholaris) is another medicinal plant used in Ayurveda. It is native to the Indian subcontinent and is also found in other parts of Asia. Saptaparna is commonly used to improve digestion and treat respiratory disorders. It is often used in the form of a powder or decoction. In terms of its physical use, Saptaparna is believed to stimulate digestion and improve the absorption of nutrients. It is also used to treat respiratory disorders such as asthma and bronchitis, as it is thought to have expectorant properties. In addition to its medicinal uses, Saptaparna is also used in traditional Ayurvedic beauty treatments for its skin-nourishing properties.

ϷϷϷ

DR. JAGADEESH PILLAI

NINETY-EIGHT
SARIVA

Sariva (सरीवा) - Hemidesmus Indicus

Sariva (Hemidesmus indicus) is another medicinal plant used in Ayurveda. It is native to the Indian subcontinent and is also found in other parts of Asia. Sariva is commonly used to improve skin health and treat fever. In terms of its physical use, Sariva is believed to have cooling and diuretic properties and is therefore often used to treat fever and other conditions characterized by excess heat in the body. It is also used to improve skin health, as it is believed to have antioxidant and anti-inflammatory properties. In addition to its medicinal uses, Sariva is also used in traditional Ayurvedic beauty treatments for its skin-nourishing properties.

NINETY-NINE
SHALAPARNI

Shalaparni (शलापर्णी) - Desmodium Gangeticum

Shalaparni, also known as Desmodium gangeticum, is an ayurvedic medicinal plant that originates from India. It is commonly used to improve strength and treat respiratory disorders such as asthma and bronchitis. In addition to its medicinal properties, Shalaparni is also known for its rejuvenating effects on the body, making it a popular choice for those seeking to improve their overall physical health and well-being.

ᙏᙏᙏ

ONE HUNDRED

SHANKHAPUSHPI

Shankhapushpi (शंखपुष्पी) - Convolvulus Pluricaulis

Shankhapushpi, or Convolvulus pluricaulis, is another ayurvedic medicinal plant that hails from India. It is commonly used to improve memory and cognitive function, and is also effective in treating anxiety and stress. Shankhapushpi is believed to have a calming effect on the mind and body, making it a popular choice for those seeking to reduce feelings of anxiety and improve their overall sense of well-being.

ONE HUNDRED AND ONE

SHANKHINI

Shankhini (शंखिनी) - Eclipta Prostrata

Shankhini, or Eclipta prostrata, is another ayurvedic medicinal plant that is native to India. It is commonly used to treat liver disorders and improve hair health. In addition to its medicinal properties, Shankhini is also known for its antioxidant and anti-inflammatory effects, making it a popular choice for those seeking to improve their overall physical health and well-being.

ONE HUNDRED AND TWO

SHATAPUSHPA

Shatapushpa (शतपुष्प) - Anethum Graveolens

Shatapushpa, or Anethum graveolens (Fennel) , is an ayurvedic medicinal plant that is native to India and the Mediterranean region. It is commonly used to improve digestion and treat respiratory disorders such as colds and coughs. In addition to its medicinal properties, Shatapushpa is also known for its carminative effects, making it a popular choice for those seeking to relieve bloating and other digestive discomforts.

ᏮᏮᏮ

ONE HUNDRED AND THREE

SHATAVARI

Shatavari (शतावरी) - Asparagus racemosus

Shatavari, or Asparagus racemosus, is an ayurvedic medicinal plant that is native to India. It is commonly used to improve reproductive and urinary health, and is also used to treat a variety of ailments such as menopause, fertility, and lactation. Shatavari is believed to have a nourishing and tonic effect on the body, making it a popular choice for those seeking to improve their overall physical health and well-being.

ⴵⴵⴵ

ONE HUNDRED AND FOUR

SHIGRU

Shigru (शिग्रु) - Moringa Oleifera

Shigru, or Moringa oleifera, is an ayurvedic medicinal plant that is native to India and other parts of Asia. It is commonly used to treat joint pain and improve digestion. In addition to its medicinal properties, Shigru is also known for its anti-inflammatory effects, making it a popular choice for those seeking to reduce inflammation and improve their overall physical health and well-being.

ONE HUNDRED AND FIVE

SHYONAKA

Shyonaka (श्योनक) - OroxylumIndicum

Shyonaka, or Oroxylum indicum, is another ayurvedic medicinal plant that is native to India. It is commonly used to improve digestion and treat respiratory disorders such as colds and coughs. In addition to its medicinal properties, Shyonaka is also believed to have a tonic effect on the body, making it a popular choice for those seeking to improve their overall physical health and well-being.

ᐅᐅᐅ

ONE HUNDRED AND SIX

SITA

Sita (Abies pindrow) - Hindi: Soya, English: Pine

Sita, or Abies pindrow, is an ayurvedic medicinal plant that is native to the Himalayan region of India. It is commonly known as "Soya" in Hindi and "Pine" in English. Sita is used to treat a variety of ailments, including respiratory disorders, wounds, and skin conditions. It is believed to have anti-inflammatory and antioxidant effects, making it a popular choice for those seeking to improve their overall physical health and well-being.

ᗞᗞᗞ

ONE HUNDRED AND SEVEN

SYONAKA

Syonaka (स्योनक) - Oroxylum Indicum

Syonaka, or Oroxylum indicum, is an ayurvedic medicinal plant that is native to India. It is commonly used to improve digestion and treat respiratory disorders such as colds and coughs. In addition to its medicinal properties, Syonaka is also believed to have a tonic effect on the body, making it a popular choice for those seeking to improve their overall physical health and well-being.

ᐅᐅᐅ

ONE HUNDRED AND EIGHT

TAGAR

Tagar (तगर) - Valeriana Wallichii

Tagar, or Valeriana wallichii, is another ayurvedic medicinal plant that is native to the Himalayan region of India. It is commonly used to treat insomnia and improve hair health. In addition to its medicinal properties, Tagar is also believed to have a calming effect on the mind and body, making it a popular choice for those seeking to reduce feelings of anxiety and improve their overall sense of well-being.

ppp

FEW MORE

APART FROM 108 PLANTS

FEW MORE ARE ADDING

FOR

REFERENCE

ONE HUNDRED AND NINE

TALISA

Talisa (तालिसा) - Abies webbiana

Talisa, or Abies webbiana, is an ayurvedic medicinal plant that is native to the Himalayan region of India. It is commonly used to improve digestion and treat respiratory disorders such as colds and coughs. In addition to its medicinal properties, Talisa is also believed to have a tonic effect on the body, making it a popular choice for those seeking to improve their overall physical health and well-being.

ONE HUNDRED AND TEN

TULASI

Tulasi (तुलसी) - Ocimum Sanctum

Tulasi, or Ocimum sanctum, is an ayurvedic medicinal plant that is native to India. It is commonly used to treat respiratory disorders such as colds and coughs, and is also believed to improve oral health. Tulasi is believed to have antiviral and antibacterial properties, making it a popular choice for those seeking to improve their overall physical health and well-being.

ONE HUNDRED AND ELEVEN

TURMERIC

Turmeric (हल्दी) - Curcuma Longa

Turmeric, or Curcuma longa, is an ayurvedic medicinal plant that is native to India and other parts of Asia. It is commonly used to treat inflammation and improve skin health. Turmeric is believed to have antioxidant and anti-inflammatory effects, making it a popular choice for those seeking to reduce inflammation and improve their overall physical health and well-being.

ᑇᑇᑇ

ONE HUNDRED AND TWELVE

VACHA

Vacha (वचा) - *Acorus Calamus*

Vacha, or Acorus calamus, is an ayurvedic medicinal plant that is native to India and other parts of Asia. It is commonly used to improve memory and treat respiratory disorders such as colds and coughs. In addition to its medicinal properties, Vacha is also believed to have a calming effect on the mind and body, making it a popular choice for those seeking to reduce feelings of anxiety and improve their overall sense of well-being.

ᗒᗒᗒ

ONE HUNDRED AND THIRTEEN

VIDANGA

Vidanga (वडिंगा) - Embelia Ribes

Vidanga, or Embelia ribes, is an ayurvedic medicinal plant that is native to India and other parts of Asia. It is commonly used to treat digestive disorders and improve oral health. Vidanga is believed to have anti-inflammatory and antioxidant effects, making it a popular choice for those seeking to reduce inflammation and improve their overall physical health and well-being.

❡❡❡

ONE HUNDRED AND FOURTEEN

YASHTIMADHU

Yashtimadhu (यष्टिमधु) - Glycyrrhiza glabra

Yashtimadhu, or Glycyrrhiza glabra, is an ayurvedic medicinal plant that is native to India and other parts of Asia. It is commonly used to treat digestive disorders and respiratory problems. Yashtimadhu is believed to have anti-inflammatory and expectorant effects, making it a popular choice for those seeking to reduce inflammation and improve their overall physical health and well-being.

❯❯❯

ONE HUNDRED AND FIFTEEN

YAVANI

Yavani (यवनी) - Trachyspermum Ammi

Yavani, or Trachyspermum ammi, is an ayurvedic medicinal plant that is native to India and other parts of Asia. It is commonly used to improve digestion and treat respiratory disorders such as colds and coughs. Yavani is believed to have a carminative effect, making it a popular choice for those seeking to relieve bloating and other digestive discomforts.

ᗞᗞᗞ

Other Books Of The Author

1. The Moments When I Met God
2. Kashiyile Theertha Pathangal
3. GURU GYAN VANI
4. Abhiprerak Gita
5. ASSI SE JAIN GHAT TAK
6. Hopelessness of Arjuna
7. The Soul and It's True Nature
8. Sense of Action (Karma)
9. Action through Wisdom
10. Action through Wisdom
11. THEORY AND PRACTICAL OF EVERY ACTION
12. LOGICAL UNDERSTANDING OF THE SUPREME
13. THE IMPERISHABLE SUPREME
14. Yatra Nishadraj se Hanuman Ghat Tak
15. Yatra Karnatak Ghat se Raja Ghat Tak
16. Yatra Pandey Ghat se Prayagraj Ghat Tak
17. Yatra Ranjendra Prasad Ghat se Dattatreya Ghat Tak
18. YaatraSindhiya Ghat se Gwaliar Ghat Tak
19. Yatra Mangala Gauri Ghat se Hanuman Gadhi Ghat Tak
20. Yatra Gaay Ghat Se Nishad Ghat Tak
21. MAA GANGA, GHATEN EVM UTSAV
22. Ganga Arti Dev Deepavali evam Any Utsav
23. Potentials of Digitalized India
24. VEDIC CONSCIOUSNESS
25. A Brief Introduction to Vedic Science
26. Kashi ke Barah Jyotirling
27. IMPACT OF MOTIVATION
28. Let's have a Milky Way Journey
29. Color Therapy in a Nutshell

❧❧❧

Contact

DR. JAGADEESH PILLAI

PhD in Vedic Science

Four Times Guinness World Record Holder

Winner of Mahatma Gandhi Vishwa Shanti Puraskar and Global Peace Ambassador

Gemology, Astro & Vastu Consultant - Spiritual Counselor

Consultant for designing World Record Ideas

Efficient Tarot Card Reader

9839093003

myrichindia@gmail.com

drjagadeeshpillai@facebook

drjagadeeshpillai@instagram

jagadeeshpillai@youtube

www. JAGADEESHPILLAI.com

❦❦❦

|| LOKAHA SAMSTHAHA SUKHINO BHAVANTU ||

• 165 •